Happy Anniversary

COMPILED BY PAUL S. NEWMAN

DESIGNS BY WULF STAPELFELDT

THE C. R. GIBSON COMPANY
NORWALK, CONNECTICUT

Copyright © MCMLXXV by
The C. R. Gibson Company, Norwalk, Connecticut
All rights reserved
Printed in the United States of America
Library of Congress Catalog Card Number: 74-83779
ISBN: 0-8378-1759-5

Memories
7

Present Joys
21

Expectations
35

Traditions and Symbols
47

Your anniversary is a special day, a milestone on the long and happy road of marriage.

Whether you are enjoying your first anniversary and looking forward with anticipation to those ahead, or at the fiftieth looking back with happy memories, it reminds you of your wedding day and the love that brought you together as man and wife. It is a time to reflect on what marriage has meant to you both.

Over hundreds of years other happy couples have commented on married life, some offering bits of wisdom, others a humorous view, and all speaking from the heart. In this book, you will find that much of what they have to say is for you to share.

Happy Anniversary!

To have and to hold from this day forward, for better for worse, for richer for poorer, in sickness, and in health, to love and to cherish, till death do us part, according to God's holy ordinance.
BOOK OF COMMON PRAYER

> We have lived and loved together
> Through many changing years;
> We have shared each other's gladness,
> And wept each other's tears.
> **CHARLES JEFFERYS**

Married couples who love each other, tell each other a thousand things without talking.
CHINESE PROVERB

If a man really loves a woman, of course he wouldn't marry her for the world if he were not quite sure that he was the best person she could by any possibility marry.
OLIVER WENDELL HOLMES

A lady of 47 who has been married 27 years and has six children knows what love really is and once described it for me like this: "Love is what you've been through with somebody."
JAMES THURBER

Mysterious is the fusion of two loving spirits: each takes the best from the other, but only to give it back again enriched with love.
ROMAIN ROLLAND

Marriage is the only known example of the happy meeting of the immovable object and the irresistible force.
OGDEN NASH

You can't appreciate home till you've left it, money till it's spent, your wife till she's joined a woman's club.
O. HENRY

> If ever two were one, then surely we.
> If ever man were lov'd by wife, then
>   thee;
> If ever wife was happy in a man,
> Compare with me ye women if you
>   can.
> ANNE BRADSTREET

The happiness of married life depends upon making small sacrifices with readiness and cheerfulness.
JOHN SELDEN

It's my old girl that advises. She has the head. But I never own to it before her. Discipline must be maintained.
CHARLES DICKENS (Bleak House)

There is no such cosy combination as man and wife.
MENANDER

Marriage is a continuous process of getting used to things you hadn't expected.
ANONYMOUS

I have learned only two things are necessary to keep one's wife happy. First, let her think she's having her way. And second, let her have it.
LYNDON B. JOHNSON

The sum which two married people owe to one another defies calculation. It is an infinite debt, which can only be discharged through all eternity.
JOHANN WOLFGANG VON GOETHE

We've been together now for forty years
An' it don't seem a day too long.
ALBERT CHERAKER

Marriage resembles a pair of shears, so joined that they can not be separated: often moving in opposite directions, yet always punishing anyone who comes between them.
SYDNEY SMITH

An ideal wife is any woman who has an ideal husband.
BOOTH TARKINGTON

Every married man should believe there's but one good wife in the world, and that's his own.
JONATHAN SWIFT

Such a large sweet fruit is a comfortable marriage, that it needs a very long summer to ripen in and then a long winter to mellow and sweeten in.
THEODORE PARKER.

"There's an advantage to being married," said the husband on his thirtieth anniversary. "You can't make a fool of yourself without knowing it quickly."

My marriage was much the most fortunate and joyous event which happened to me in my whole life.
WINSTON CHURCHILL

I have enjoyed the happiness of this world; I have lived and loved.
FRIEDRICH VON SCHILLER

After his wedding the author Arthur Kober sent the following telegram to the regular players at his weekly poker club, "Sorry I can't join you tonight as there is no way of bettering the perfect hand I am now holding."

Not caged, my bird, my shy, sweet bird,
But nested - nested!
HUBBERTON LULHAM

Love does not consist in gazing at each other but in looking outward together in the same direction. There is no comradeship except through union in the same high effort.
ANTOINE DE SAINT-EXUPERY

There is no more lovely, friendly and charming relationship, communion or company than a good marriage.
MARTIN LUTHER

To Mamie,
For never-failing help since 1916 — in calm and in stress, in dark days and in bright.
Love — Ike
Christmas 1955

DWIGHT D. EISENHOWER
(Message engraved on a gold medallion, as a Christmas gift to his wife, December 25, 1955)

At their twentieth anniversary, the couple was asked if they remembered the first meal the bride cooked.

"Of course," said Anita. "I'll always remember it because Herb helped with it."

"How sweet," said one of their friends. "What did Herb do — set the table or make the salad dressing?"

"Neither," replied Anita. "When I burned the pot roast, I tried to pull it off the stove. It fell in the dessert and started a fire. Herb put it out by pouring the soup over it."

Every man who is high up loves to think he has done it all himself; and the wife smiles, and lets it go at that. It's only our joke. Every woman knows that.
JAMES BARRIE

He came into my life as the warm wind of spring had awakened flowers, as the April showers awaken the earth. My love for him was an unchanging love, high and deep, free and faithful, strong as death. Each year I learned to love him more and more. I think of the days and years we spent together with gratitude, for God has been kind and generous in letting me love him.
ANNA CHENNAULT

How much the wife is dearer than the bride.
LORD LYTTLETON

I chose my wife, as she did her wedding gown, not for a fine glossy surface, but such qualities as would wear well.
OLIVER GOLDSMITH

The reason why lovers are never weary of one another is this — they are always talking of themselves.
FRANÇOIS, DUE DE LA ROCHEFOUCAULD

One year of Joy, another of Comfort, and all the rest of content, make the married Life happy.
THOMAS FULLER

Won 1880. One 1884.
Inscription on ring given to his wife
by WILLIAM JENNINGS BRYAN

Remember the nightingales which sing only some months in the spring, but commonly are silent when they have hatched their eggs, as if their mirth were turned into care for their young ones. Yet all the Molestations of Marriage are abundantly recompensed with the comforts which God bestoweth on them who make a wise choice of a wife.
THOMAS FULLER

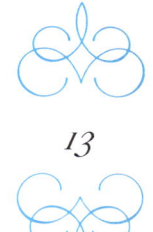

13

In vain is that man born fortunate, if he be unfortunate in his marriage.
ANNE DACIER

In three things I was beautified, and stood up beautiful before the Lord and men: the concord of brethren, and friendship of neighbours, and a woman and her husband that walk together in agreement.
ECCLESIASTICUS 25:1

In my Sunday School class there was a beautiful little girl with golden curls. I was smitten with her once and still am.
HARRY S. TRUMAN

It takes a man twenty-five years to learn to be married; it's a wonder women have the patience to wait for it.
CLARENCE B. KELLAND

No, I haven't any formula. I can just say it's been a very happy experience . . . a successful marriage, I think, gets happier as the years go by.
DWIGHT D. EISENHOWER, ON HIS 43RD WEDDING ANNIVERSARY

He credited her with a number of virtues, of the existence of which her conduct and conversation had given but limited indications. But, then, lovers have a proverbial power of balancing inverted pyramids, going to sea in sieves, and successfully performing kindred feats impossible to a faithless and unbelieving generation.
L. MALET

We bachelors laugh and show our teeth, but you married men laugh till your hearts ache.
GEORGE HERBERT

At his tenth anniversary, a man was asked if he and his wife ever had any differences of opinion.

"Many, many!" he nodded. "And important ones!"

"Then how come," asked his friend. "You seem to get along so well?"

"I never tell her about them."

When Erica Cotterill began writing to George Bernard Shaw in 1906, it began a long correspondence — on her part — telling of her profound love and asking for literary advice. In April 1908, after describing to her how to obtain a literary contract, he continued . . .

Now that I have taught you some respect for business and the law, let me assure you that marriage is more sacred than either, and that unless you are prepared to treat my wife with absolute loyalty, you will be hurled into outer darkness for ever.

The privilege of pawing me, such as it is, is hers exclusively.

She has to tolerate worshipping females whose efforts to conceal the fact that they take no interest in her are perfunctory, and who bore her to distraction with their adoration of me; but it is my business to see that her patience is not abused . . . Whenever I get anything in the nature of a love letter, I hand it straight to Charlotte . . .

Love consists in this, that two solitudes protect and touch and greet each other.
RAINER MARIA RILKE

Between a man and his wife nothing ought to rule but love.
WILLIAM PENN

If it hadn't been for my wife, I couldn't have stood married life.
DON HEROLD

There is something about a wedding-gown prettier than in any other gown in the world.
DOUGLAS JERROLD

I could not have lived my life without Alice. If my wife had been hurt, how could I have had the strength to go on?
JUSTICE LOUIS BRANDEIS

"What's your formula for a successful marriage," the husband was asked on his 32nd anniversary.
"Never show your worst side to your better half."

Whenever I hear people say they have lived together twenty-five years and never had the least difference, I wonder whether they have not had a good deal of indifference.
ROBERT COLLYER

"Communication," said the husband on his tenth anniversary, "is the key to a happy marriage. When I talk, she listens. When she talks, I listen. And when we both talk — the neighbors listen."

There is more of good nature than of good sense at the bottom of most marriages.
HENRY DAVID THOREAU

The reason that husbands and wives do not understand each other is because they belong to different sexes.
DOROTHY DIX

You are my true and honorable wife,
Dear as the ruddy drops that warm my heart.
THOMAS GRAY

Mutual love, the crown of all our bliss.
JOHN MILTON

To church in the morning, and there saw a wedding in the church, which I have not seen in many a day; and the young people so merry one with another! and strange to see what delight we married people have to see these poor fools decoyed into our condition, every man and woman gazing and smiling at them.
SAMUEL PEPYS

A good marriage is that in which each appoints the other guardian of his solitude.
RAINER MARIA RILKE

Teacher, tender comrade, wife,
A fellow-farer true through life.
ROBERT LOUIS STEVENSON

Love looks through a telescope; envy, through a microscope.
HENRY WHEELER SHAW

"You mean in all the years you've always had the last words when you argue with Lily?"

"Yes, and they're always the same ones — 'You're right'."

Husband and wife come to look alike at last.
OLIVER WENDELL HOLMES

I should like to see any kind of a man, distinguishable from a gorilla, that some good and even pretty woman could not shape a husband out of.
OLIVER WENDELL HOLMES

Marriage is that relation between man and woman in which the independence is equal, the dependence mutual, and the obligation reciprocal.
L. K. ANSPACHER

Just at closing time, a middle-aged man rushed into the office of the town clerk.

"Quick! Quick," he exclaimed. "Find my marriage certificate."

"But we're closing," said the clerk, putting on his coat.

"You've got to help me," said man, desperately grabbing the clerk's lapels. "It's a matter of life and death!"

The clerk sighed, got the man's name and started his search. Five minutes later, he showed the man his marriage certificate.

"Thank goodness," grinned the man. "We were married June 6th . . . I still have a day left to find an anniversary present."

If you have the good luck to find a modest wife, you should prostrate yourself before the Tarpeian threshold, and sacrifice a heifer with gilded horns to Juno.
JUVENAL

Bone of my bones, and flesh of my flesh.
GENESIS 2:23

A married man forms married habits and becomes dependent on marriage just as a sailor becomes dependent on the sea.
GEORGE BERNARD SHAW

Some husbands have no talent for remembering anniversaries, while with others it's a gift.

According to the Emily Post of the last half of the 1800's, Mrs. M. E. W. Sherwood, "The twentieth anniversary of one's wedding is never celebrated. It is considered very unlucky to do so. The Scotch think one or the other will die within the year if the twentieth anniversary is even alluded to." She goes on to describe a "typical" evening celebration of the twenty-fifth, "In savage communities (the wife) would dig the earth, wait upon her lord, and stand behind him while he eats; in the modern silver wedding he helps her to fried oysters and champagne, and stands while she sits."

Marriage has many pains, but celibacy has no pleasures.
SAMUEL JOHNSON

Husband: "Even though we were married nineteen years ago, I still remember that beautiful moment when I proposed to you, darling, on your back porch."
Wife: "But we lived on the ninth floor of an apartment house!"

Love, then hath every bliss in store;
'Tis friendship and 'tis something more.
Each other every wish they give;
Not to know love is not to live.
     JOHN GAY

The one word above all others that makes marriage successful is 'ours.'
     ROBERT QUILLEN

The Little Poem of Life

I;—
Thou;—
We;—
They;—
Small words, but mighty.
In their span
Are bound the life and hopes of man.
For, first, his thoughts of his own self are full;
Until another comes his heart to rule.
For them, life's best is centred round their love;
Till younger lives come all their love to prove.
     JOHN OXENHAM

> God, the best maker of all marriages,
> Combine yours hearts in one.
> **WILLIAM SHAKESPEARE**

> Husbands are things wives have to get used to
>   putting up with,
> And with whom they breakfast with and sup with.
> They interfere with the disciplines of nurseries,
> And forget anniversaries,
> And when they have been particularly remiss
> They think they can cure everything with a great big kiss.
> **OGDEN NASH**

> I am now I believe fixed at this Seat with an agreeable Consort for Life and hope to find more happiness in retirement than I ever experienced amidst a wide and bustling World.
> **GEORGE WASHINGTON**, September 20, 1759
> Mount Vernon

> With thee all toils are sweet; each clime hath charms; earth - sea alike - our world within our arms!
> **GEORGE GORDON, LORD BYRON**

22

> A happy marriage is a new beginning of life, a new starting point for happiness and usefulness.
> **A. P. STANLEY**

> No cord nor cable can so forcibly draw, or hold so fast, as love can do with a twined thread.
> **ROBERT BURTON**

To love means to decide independently to live with an equal partner, and to subordinate oneself to the formation of a new subject, a "we."
FRITZ KUNKEL

The crowning glory of loving and being loved is that the pair make no real progress; however far they have advanced into the enchanted land during the day they must start again from the frontier the next morning.
JAMES BARRIE

While Winston Churchill was campaigning for re-election, a voter from the other party tried to heckle him. "May we expect you to continue serving the powerful interest that controls your vote?"

Churchill growled, "I'll thank you to keep my wife's name out of this!"

No angel she; she hath no budding wings;
   No mystic halo circles her bright hair:
But lo! the infinite grace of little things,
   Wrought for dear love's sake, makes her very fair.
JAMES B. KENYON

The aim of marriage should be to give the best years of your life to the spouse who makes them the best.

A man asked the airline official at the boarding gate, "Have I got enough time to say goodby to my wife?"

"That depends, sir. How long have been married?"

This is a great day, my darling, the day that gave you to me fifteen years ago. You were very precious to me then, you are still more precious to me now. In having each other then, we were well off; but poor compared to what we have now with the children.
   I kiss you, my darling wife — and those little rascals.
MARK TWAIN
(note to his wife)

Love makes those young whom age does chill
And whom he finds young keeps young still.
WILLIAM CARTWRIGHT

There is not earthly happiness exceeding that of a reciprocal satisfaction in the conjugal state.
H. GILES

The most welcome surprise you can give your wife on your anniversary is to remember it.

No happiness is like unto it, no love so great as that of man and wife, no such comfort as a sweet wife.
ROBERT BURTON

Two persons who have chosen each other out of all the species, with the design to be each other's mutual comfort and entertainment, have, in that action, bound themselves to be goodhumored, affable, discreet, forgiving, patient, and joyful, with respect to each other's frailties and perfections, to the end of their lives.
JOSEPH ADDISON

> I want (who does not want?) a wife,
>   Affectionate and fair,
> To solace all the woes of life,
>   And all its joys to share;
> Of temper sweet, of yielding will,
>   Of firm, yet placid mind,
> With all my faults to love me still,
>   With sentiment refin'd.
> JOHN QUINCY ADAMS

"Now you're approaching your tenth anniversary," a friend asked. "What do you think is the key to your successful marriage, Harry?"

"We divide our responsibilities. Zelma makes all the minor decisions — what kind of a house we'll buy, where our kids'll go to school, do we get a new car, should I ask for a raise."

"And your responsibilities?"

"I make the major decisions — should we drill for oil off our American coastline, do we stay in the United Nations, how much should we spend for national defense, stuff like that."

> My heart, I fain would ask thee
>   What then is Love? say on.
> "Two souls with but a single thought,
>   Two hearts that beat as one."
> JOSEF VON MUNCH-BELLINGHAUSEN

I should like to know what is the proper function of women, if it is not to make reasons for husbands to stay home, and still stronger reasons for bachelors to go out.
GEORGE ELIOT

On the way to the airport after the wedding, the bride asked her husband, a bachelor for forty years, if he had their plane tickets. He confidently reached into his pocket . . . and then saw that out of habit, he had bought just one ticket. "Incredible! Just one ticket. You know, dear, I've been married only an hour and already I've forgotten all about myself."

My fairest, my espous'd, my latest found,
Heaven's last best gift, my ever new delight!
                    JOHN MILTON

The plainest man that can convince a woman that he is really in love with her has done more to make her in love with him than the handsomest man, if he can produce no such conviction. For the love of woman is a shoot, not a seed, and flourishes most vigorously only when ingrafted on that love which is rooted in the breast of another.
                    CHARLES CALEB COLTON

"Now that you're married," enthused the eager insurance agent, "you'll want to increase your insurance —"

"Why?" interrupted the husband. "My wife doesn't seem dangerous."

Deceive not thyself by over-expecting happiness in the married state . . . Look not therein for contentment greater than God will give, or a creature in this world can receive, namely, to be free from all inconveniences . . . Marriage is not like the hill of Olympus, wholly clear, without clouds.
                    THOMAS FULLER

... for your brother and my sister no sooner met but they looked; no sooner looked but they loved; no sooner loved but they sighed; no sooner sighed but they asked one another the reason; no sooner knew the reason but they sought the remedy: and in these degrees have they made a pair of stairs to marriage ...
WILLIAM SHAKESPEARE

Courtship to marriage is but as the music in the playhouse till the curtain's drawn.
WILLIAM CONGREVE

> How could I, blest with thee, long nights employ,
> And how with thee the longest day enjoy!
TIBULLUS

The bonds of matrimony are like any other bonds — they mature slowly.
PETER DE VRIES

A wife is essential to great longevity; she is the receptacle of half a man's cares, and two-thirds of his ill-humor.
CHARLES READE

The only present love demands is love.
JOHN GAY

We attract hearts by the qualities we display: we retain them by the qualities we possess.
JEAN SUARD

As the couple were about to leave on their honeymoon, one older bridesmaid whispered sage advice to the bride, "If you want to keep your husband at home — ask him to take you some place."

The world well tried — the sweetest thing in life
Is the unclouded welcome of a wife.
                               N. P. WILLIS

As a great part of the uneasiness of matrimony arises from mere trifles, it would be wise in every young married man to enter into an agreement with his wife that in all disputes the party who was most convinced they were right would always surrender the victory. By this means both would be more forward to give up the cause.
                             HENRY FIELDING

Memo: not to adulterize my time by absenting myself from my wife.
                           SAMUEL TAYLOR COLERIDGE

Try praising your wife even if it terrifies her at first.

Well-married a man is winged: ill-matched, he is shackled.
                         HENRY WARD BEECHER

Enjoy your husband, but never think you know him thoroughly.
                         LADYBIRD JOHNSON

She who dwells with me, who I have loved
With such communion, that no place on earth
Can ever be a solitude for me.
                    WILLIAM WORDSWORTH

  A good wife is a generous gift
       bestowed upon him who fears the Lord;
Be he rich or poor, his heart is content,
       and a smile is ever on his face.
               ECCLESIASTICUS 26:3, 4

He who marries is like the Doge (of Venice) who marries the Adriatic — he doesn't know what's in it: treasures, pearls, monsters, unknown storms.
                    HEINRICH HEINE

Whatever woman may cast her lot with mine, should any ever do so, it is my intention to do all in my power to make her happy and contented; and there is nothing I can imagine that would make me more unhappy than to fail in that effort.
                ABRAHAM LINCOLN

If 20 years were to be erased and I were to be presented with the same choice again under the same circumstances I would act precisely as I did then . . . Perhaps I needed her even more in those searing lonely moments when I — I alone knew in my heart what my decision must be. I have needed her all these 20 years. I love her and need her now. I always will.
        DUKE OF WINDSOR, on 20th anniversary of his marriage to Wallis Warfield Simpson for whom he abdicated as Edward VIII of England.

Of all my loves the last, for here after I shall glow with passion for no other woman.
HORACE

The owner of the local doughnut shop was about to close up, as the rain came down in buckets late one night.

"Wait!" shouted a man. He ran, leaning against the strong wind, the rain battering his raincoat that he clutched to keep closed. "I need two doughnuts."

"Two? You came out on a night like this for just two doughnuts?"

"Right. Norma wanted one, so I figured I might as well have one, too."

"Is Norma your wife?"

"Who else," he sighed, wiping the rain from his face. "Do you think my mother would send me out on a night like this?"

> She is a winsome wee thing,
> She is a handsome wee thing,
> She is a lo'esome wee thing,
>   This sweet wee wife o' mine.
ROBERT BURNS

Our state cannot be severed; we are one,
One flesh; to lose thee were to lose myself.
JOHN MILTON

God has set the type of marriage everywhere throughout creation . . . Every creature seeks its perfection in another . . . The very heavens and earth picture it to us.
MARTIN LUTHER

It's a long time ago, my darling, but the 33 years have been really profitable to us, and is worth more each year than it was the year before. And so it will be always, dearest old Sweetheart of my youth.
    Good night and sleep well.
MARK TWAIN
(note sent up to his wife's room in Italy where she lay seriously ill.)

A man's best possession is a sympathetic wife.
EURIPIDES

Keep your eyes wide open before marriage, half shut afterwards.
BENJAMIN FRANKLIN

A wife has to thank God her husband has faults; a husband without faults is a dangerous observer.
LORD HALIFAX

A successful marriage is an edifice that must be rebuilt every day.
ANDRE MAUROIS

The secret of happy marriage is simple: Just keep on being as polite to one another as you are to your best friends.
R. QUILLEN

The motto of chivalry is also the motto of wisdom: to serve all, but love only one.
HONORE DE BALZAC

A heaven on earth I have won by wooing thee.
WILLIAM SHAKESPEARE

We should marry to please ourselves, not other people.
ISAAC BICKERSTAFFE

Affections, like the conscience, are rather to be led than drawn; and 'tis to be feared, they that marry where they do not love, will love where they do not marry.
THOMAS FULLER

A person's character is but half formed till after wedlock.
C. SIMMONS

"I never knew," sighed the bride, as she unwrapped her sixth coffee pot, "how much people thought alike till I started opening our wedding presents."

Marriages are made in heaven, but they are lived on earth.
NATHAN H. GIST

To love is to place our happiness in the happiness of another.
BARON GOTTFRIED VON LEIBNITZ

But, to the charms which I adore,
'Tis religion to be true!
RICHARD BRINSLEY SHERIDAN

The first bond of society is marriage.
CICERO

Whoever says marriage is a fifty-fifty proposition doesn't know the half of it.

> He is the half part of a blessed man,
> Left to be finished by such a she;
> And she a fair divided excellence,
> Whose fullness of perfection lies in him.
> WILLIAM SHAKESPEARE

Best image of myself and dearer half.
JOHN MILTON

> For in what stupid age or nation
> Was marriage ever out of fashion?
> SAMUEL BUTLER

Of all the home remedies, a good wife is the best.
KIN HUBBARD

The man and the woman who can laugh at their love, who can kiss with smiles and embrace with chuckles, will outlast in mutual affection all the throat-lumpy, cow-eyed couples of their acquaintance. Nothing lives on so fresh and evergreen as the love with a funny bone.
GEORGE JEAN NATHAN

Love one human being purely and warmly, and you will love all ... The heart in this heaven, like the sun in its course, sees nothing, from the dewdrop to the ocean, but a mirror which it brightens, and arms, and fills.
CONRAD RICHTER

If you would be loved, love and be lovable.
BENJAMIN FRANKLIN

If a husband is smart enough to play second fiddle, he'll have harmony at home.

"I've been married forty-two years and not regretted a single day of it," said the husband on his anniversary. "And that day was April 29th, nineteen hundred and ..."

Expectations

The highest happiness on earth is marriage. Every man who is happy is a successful man even if he has failed in everything else.
WILLIAM LYON PHELPS

The test of a happily married — and a wise woman — is whether she can say, "I love you" far oftener than she asks, "Do you love me?"
DOROTHY DAYTON

    At their thirtieth anniversary, the husband, looking at the wife he adored, said, "I don't know how you can think of going on with me. You keep getting more attractive, but me . . . just getting older with less hair."
    "So what?" she replied, patting his cheek. "It just means in the future I won't get in your hair as much."

The only thing that can hallow marriage is love, and the only genuine marriage is that which is hallowed by love.
COUNT LEO TOLSTOY

It is not marriage that fails; it is the people that fail. All that marriage does is to show people up.
HARRY EMERSON FOSDICK

An intelligent wife sees through a husband, an understanding wife sees him through.

It is always better to have your wife with you than after you.

It takes years to marry completely two hearts, even of the most loving and well-assorted. A happy wedlock is a long falling in love. Young persons think love belongs only to the brown-haired and crimson-cheeked. So it does for its beginning. But the golden marriage is a part of love which the Bridal day knows nothing of.

A perfect and complete marriage, where wedlock is everything you could ask and the ideal of marriage becomes actual, is not common, perhaps as rare as perfect personal beauty. Men and women are married fractionally, now a small fraction, then a large fraction. Very few are married totally, and they only after some forty or fifty years of gradual approach and experiment.

Such a large and sweet fruit is a complete marriage that it needs a long summer to ripen in, and then a long winter to mellow and season it. But a real, happy marriage of love and judgment between a noble man and woman is one of the things so very handsome that if the sun were, as the Greek poets fabled, a God, he might stop the world and hold it still now and then in order to look all day long on some example therof, and feast his eyes on such a spectacle.
THEODORE PARKER

Change everything, except your loves.
VOLTAIRE

The supreme happiness of life is the conviction of being loved for yourself, or, more correctly, being loved in spite of yourself.
VICTOR HUGO

We are shaped and fashioned by what we love.
JOHANN WOLFGANG VON GOETHE

So long as the emotional feelings between the couple are right, so long as there is mutual trust and love, their bodies will invariably make the appropriate responses.
DR. DAVID R. MACE,

      Love has the patience
         To endure
     The fault it sees
          But cannot cure.
EDGAR GUEST

At her fiftieth wedding anniversary, the wife was asked if she had ever thought of divorcing her husband. "Divorce him? No. Shoot him — yes!"

The kindest and the happiest pair will find occasion to forbear; and something, every day they live, to pity and perhaps forgive.
WILLIAM COWPER

True love is eternal, infinite, and always like itself. It is equal and pure, without violent demonstrations: it is seen with white hairs and is always young in the heart.
HONORE DE BALZAC

A man reserves his greatest and deepest love not for the woman in whose company he finds himself electrified and enkindled but for that one in whose company he may feel tenderly drowsy.
GEORGE JEAN NATHAN

At their seventy-fifth anniversary, someone asked the aged husband, "Why do you think the Lord let you reach this day?"

"To prove our patience with each other," he replied.

> Dawn love is silver,
>   Wait for the west:
> Old love is gold love —
>   Old love is best.
> KATHERINE LEE BATES

Somewhere there waiteth in this world of ours
    For one lone soul, another lonely soul,
Each choosing each through all the weary hours,
    And meeting strangely at one sudden goal,
Then blend they, like green leaves with golden flowers,
    Into one beautiful perfect whole;
And life's long night is ended, and the way
Lies open onward to eternal day.
EDWIN ARNOLD

A great proportion of the wretchedness which has embittered married life, has originated in a negligence of trifles. Connubial happiness is a thing of too fine a texture to be handled roughly. It is a sensitive plant, which will not bear even the touch of unkindness; a delicate flower, which indifference will chill and suspicion blast. It must be watered by the showers of tender affection, expanded by the cheering glow of kindness, and guarded by the impregnable barrier of unshaken confidence. Thus matured, it will bloom with fragrance in every season of life, and sweeten even the loneliness of declining years.
THOMAS SPRAT

The heart that loves is always young.
GREEK PROVERB

A happy marriage is a long conversation that always seems too short.
ANDRE MAUROIS

   Let me not to the marriage of true
      minds
   Admit impediments. Love is not love
   Which alters when it alteration finds,
   Or bends with the remover to remove:
   O, no! it is an ever-fixed mark,
   That looks on tempests and is never shaken;
   It is the star to every wandering bark,
   Whose worth's unknown, although his height be taken.
   Love's not Time's fool, though rosy lips and cheeks
   Within his bending sickle's compass come;
   Love alters not with his brief hours and weeks,
   But bears it out even to the edge of doom.
   If this be error, and upon me prov'd,
   I never writ, nor no man ever lov'd.
WILLIAM SHAKESPEARE

It takes patience to appreciate domestic bliss; volatile spirits prefer unhappiness.
GEORGE SANTAYANA

A prominent man, when asked what other person he would rather be than himself, replied, "My wife's second husband." That was true love and beautiful loyalty.
NATHAN H. GIST

A good wife is like the ivy which beautifies the building to which it clings, twining tendrils more lovingly as time converts the ancient edifice into ruins.
SAMUEL JOHNSON

> Thus let me hold thee to my heart,
> And every care resign:
> And we shall never, never part,
> My life — my all that's mine!
> OLIVER GOLDSMITH

When the one man loves the one woman and the one woman loves the one man, the very angels desert heaven and come and sit in that house and sing for joy.
BRAHMA

What greater thing is there for two human souls than to feel that they are joined for life — to strengthen each other in all labor, to rest on each other in all sorrow, to minister to each other in all pain, to be one with each other in silent, unspeakable memories at the moment of the last parting.
GEORGE ELIOT

An archaeologist is the best husband any woman can have: the older she gets, the more interested he is in her.
AGATHA CHRISTIE
(Wife of an Archaeologist)

> Will you love me in December as you do in May?
> Will you love me in the good old fashioned way?
> JAMES J. WALKER

> Serene will be our days and bright
> And happy will our nature be,
> When love is an unerring light,
> And joy its own security.
> — WILLIAM WORDSWORTH

A sixty-year-old man puffed down the platform and just made the 8:14. "Can't wait till I retire next month."

"What'll you do?" asked his friend, who had watched him "just" make that train every day for many years.

"I'm telling my wife to stop frying my eggs on both sides. For the rest of my marriage, I want them as I prefer them — sunny side up."

"Why didn't you tell your wife that before?"

"Never had the time."

> If two stand shoulder to shoulder against the gods,
> Happy together, the gods themselves are helpless
> Against them while they stand so.
> — MAXWELL ANDERSON

A couple were arguing, when the husband interrupted, "We can't go on like this. We should get professional help."

"You're right," said his wife. "That's the way to save our marriage. A marriage counselor can tell us what our problem is."

"Will you make an appointment for us —"

"Sure, dear," replied his wife. "And you don't even have to go. I can speak for us both."

Marriage is a status of antagonistic cooperation. In such a status, necessarily, centripetal and centrifugal forces are continuously at work, and the measure of its success obviously depends on the extent to which the centripetal forces are predominant.
    FEDERAL JUDGE JOHN M. WOOLSEY

> The joys of marriage are the heaven on earth,
> Life's paradise, great princess, the soul's quiet,
> Sinews of concord, earthly immortality,
> Eternity of pleasures.
>   JOHN FORD

True love is the ripe fruit of a lifetime.
    ALPHONSE DE LAMARTINE

The true one of youth's love, proving a faithful help-meet in those years when the dream of life is over, and we live in its realities.
    ROBERT SOUTHEY

> Thus hand in hand through life we'll go;
> Its checkered paths of joy and woe
>   With cautious steps we'll tread.
>   NATHANIEL COTTON

A wife is one who shares her husband's thoughts, incorporates his heart in love with hers, and crowns him with her trust. She is God's remedy for loneliness and God's reward for all the toil of life.
    HENRY VAN DYKE

No man ever forgot the visitation of that power to his heart and brain, which created all things anew; which was the dawn in him of music, poetry and art; which made the face of nature radiant with purple light, the morning and the night varied enchantments; . . . when he became all eye when one was present, and all memory when one was gone.
RALPH WALDO EMERSON

A man loved by a beautiful and virtuous woman, carries with him a talisman that renders him invulnerable; every one feels that such a one's life has a higher value than that of others.
MADAME DUDEVANT

'But true Love is a durable fire
In the mind ever burning;
Never sick, never old, never dead,
From itself never turning.'
SIR WALTER RALEGH

Let every husband stay a lover true,
And every wife remain a sweetheart too.
ANONYMOUS

Success in marriage is much more than finding the right person; it is a matter of being the right person.
B. R. BRICKNER

As your wedding ring wears,
You'll wear off your cares.
THOMAS FULLER

Young love is a flame, very pretty, often very hot and fierce, but still only light and flickering. The love of the older and disciplined heart is as coals, deep-burning, unquenchable.
HENRY WARD BEECHER

> The married man may bear his yoke with ease,
> Secure at once himself and Heav'n to please;
> And pass his inoffensive hours away,
> In bliss all night, and innocence all day;
> Tho' fortune change, his constant spouse remains,
> Augments his joys, or mitigates his pains.
> ALEXANDER POPE

A married man falling into misfortune is more apt to retrieve his situation in the world than a single one, chiefly because his spirits are soothed and retrieved by domestic endearments, and his self respect kept alive by finding that although all abroad be darkness and humiliation, yet there is a little world of love at home over which he is a monarch.
JEREMY TAYLOR

With all thy faults, I love thee still.
WILLIAM COWPER

True love is always young in the heart.
HONORE DE BALZAC

No man knows what the wife of his bosom is — what a ministering angel she is, until he has gone with her through the fiery trials of this world.
WASHINGTON IRVING

We are all born for love: it is the principle of existence and its only end.
BENJAMIN DISRAELI

> Love ever gives,
> Forgives, outlives,
> And ever stands
> With open hands.
> And, while it lives,
> It gives.
> For this is Love's perogative —
> To give and give and give.
> JOHN OSENHAM

Love, in the divine alchemy of life, transmutes all duties into privileges, all responsibilities into joys.
WILLIAM GEORGE JORDAN

I like not only to be loved, but also to be told that I am loved. I am not sure that you are of the same kind. But the realm of silence is large enough beyond the grave. This is the world of light and speech, and I shall take leave to tell you that you are very dear.
GEORGE ELIOT

> The light of love
>   shines over all,
> Of love, that says
>   not mine and thine,
> But ours, for ours
>   is thine and mine.
> HENRY WADSWORTH LONGFELLOW

authority. Greek and Roman brides wore red veils, early Christian white or purple. Even today, in some countries, the groom never sees his bride's face until they are married.

The WEDDING CAKE goes back to the Roman custom of breaking a thin loaf over the bride's head. Wheat symbolized fertility to the Romans and the guests grabbed for the crumbs as tokens of good luck. An ancient English custom had the bride and groom trying to kiss over a pile of little cakes that numbered over a hundred and rose as a humorous barrier between them.

Following is a list of the wedding anniversaries in chronological order, with their respective symbols. The anniversaries most often celebrated are marked with a star. Symbols repeated by a lesser number of authorities are in parentheses.

*First — paper
 Second — cotton, calico
 Third — leather
 Fourth — fruit, flowers, books, (silk, linen)
*Fifth — wood
 Sixth — candy, sugar, iron
 Seventh — wool, copper, brass, bronze
 Eighth — rubber, electrical appliances, (bronze, pottery)
 Ninth — pottery, willow, china
*Tenth — tin, aluminum
 Eleventh — steel
 Twelfth — linen, silk, nylon
 Thirteenth — lace
 Fourteenth — ivory
*Fifteenth — crystal
*Twentieth — china
*Twenty-fifth — silver

*Thirtieth — pearl
 Thirty-fifth — coral, jade
*Fortieth — ruby
 Forty-fifth — sapphire
*Fiftieth — golden
 Fifty-fifth — emerald
 Seventy-fifth — diamond

Note. — Some authorities list a sixtieth anniversary with the diamond as a symbol. One authority lists the sixtieth with the star sapphire as the symbol: but it is not often celebrated.

BEATRICE PLUMB

GIFT SUGGESTIONS FOR WEDDING ANNIVERSARIES

FIRST—*Paper.*—Albums; artificial flowers; books, including account, budget, cook, diary, gardening, labels, stamps, etc.; calendars; card decks; curtains; etchings; initialed napkins and book matches; lamp shades; photographs; sheet music; subscriptions to periodicals; stationery; paper tablecloth, napkins, cups, plates and spoons; water color prints; and a new twenty-dollar bill, rolled in thin white tissue paper to resemble a cigarette, and labeled, "Do Not Smoke!" and put in pack with real cigarettes.

SECOND—*Cotton.*—Aprons; bathmat set; beach towels; broadcloth shirts; brunch coat; cotton poplin smock; cotton terry cloth robe; cotton flannelette lounging robe; chintz (glazed) mitt and apron set; dresser scarves; garment bags; house dresses; ironing board cover set; muslin sheets; pillow cases; pot holders; shoe bags; slip covers; tablecloths; thread kit; towels; yard goods; a homemade patchwork quilt, or embroidered, tufted twin bedspreads.

THIRD—*Leather.*—Any leather-bound album or book for addresses, autographs, diary, photos, snapshots, mementos, foreign stamps, etc.; alligator belt; memo pad; billfold; book covers and markers; sets of leather-bound classics; brief bag; car seat covers; card case; change purse; carry-all shoulder bag for camera and gadgets; Florentine leather jewel case or trinket box; key case; leather cap, gloves, jacket, storm boots; picnic leather zip case, containing vacuum bottles, plastic cups and sandwich box; Pullman moccasin slippers in case; sewing kit; zipper ring binder; traveler's game set.

FOURTH—*Fruit, Flowers, and Books.*—Citrus fruit in plain box or fancy basket; crystallized fruit; assorted fruit jams, jellies, conserves; canned fruit and fruit juices; cut flowers; glass bowl of imported French paper-white narcissus; potted flowering plants or shrubs; a dozen choice rose bushes, planted, with a supply of fertilizer; artifical flowers for tablepiece or dress accessories; atlas; Bible; cookbook; dictionary; books relating to his or her business or hobby; personal book plates; book ends.

FIFTH—*Wood.*—Baskets for flowers, sewing, or firewood; birchwood novelties; log cabin bird house; bowls for salad, nuts, etc.; clocks; clothes trees; curio cabinet for collector's pieces; hair brush sets, with satin wood backs; hardwood combination coat and trouser hanger; mahogany tier lamp table; luggage rack; lapboard, initialed; Ming trees; personalized pencils; pipe holders; shadow boxes; salad set; service tray, carved or hand-painted; spruce shoe shine box; copies of Early American solid pine letter racks, pipe racks, desk boxes, spice chests, and miniature cradle; tea wagon; garden or porch furniture made of wood.

SIXTH—*Candy, Sugar, and Iron.*—Boxes and tins of candy; sweet novelties, as candy imitations of cigars, cigarettes, coins; homemade taffy, fudge, and butterscotch; boxes of all types of sugar; andirons; cooking ware; dachshund cast-iron foot-scraper; gas hot plate; house number and design in wrought iron; paperweight; horseshoes; magnets; old iron lanterns, locks, coffers, fire screens, tools, and cooking utensils.

SEVENTH—*Wool, Copper, Brass, and Bronze.*—Afghan; angora sweater; bed jacket; blankets; cashmere cardigan; cashmere man-size colored scarf; checked man's shirt; wool flannel robe; fringed throw; gloves; golfing argyles; hand-loomed wool square scarf; knitting wool; wool-filled comforter; skating cap and gloves; wool tartan blanket robe in plastic zip carrying case; copper, brass, and bronze andirons; antiques; archway lanterns; bells; book ends; clocks; curtain rod and rings; desk sets; figurines; flower bowls; folding fire screens; gooseneck table lamp; gypsy kettles for hanging plants; lamps; frames; sundial; trays; embossed brass treasure box; teakettle on tripod; wood holder for hearth; three-fold miniature picture frames in solid brass; copper chafing dish, banded in brass; three-piece dresser set in jeweler's bronze.

EIGHTH—*Rubber, Electrical Appliances, and Bronze.*—Rubber apron; bath mat; bathing cap; beach ball; surf animal; tire; box of assorted rubber bands; boots; doll; gloves; gardener's kneeling pad; garden hose; hot water bottle; initial doormat of rough weather rubber; invalid's cushion; man's rain jacket, pants, and cape; any electrical household specialty; baby bottle warmer; corn popper; curling irons; dish washer; door chimes; electric mixer; fan; flashlight; purse-size flashlight key ring; grill; hair drier; heat lamp; iron; percolator; radio; shaving razor;

television; toaster; travel iron in case; vacuum cleaner; phonograph; waffle iron; washing machine; electric blanket. (See seventh anniversary for bronze.)

NINTH—*Pottery and Willow.*—Any art pottery souvenir, curio, and antique; ash tray; candy dish; cigarette box; quaint characters or animals done in pottery; collector's jugs or steins; fern jardinere; imported figurines; table lamps; tea and toast sets; casserole set of brown glazed pottery; blue willow ware; baskets of all types; porch furniture of wicker, bamboo, or rattan.

TENTH—*Tin and Aluminum.*—Tinware, plain, painted or enameled; batter whip; basting spoon; bread pan; candlesticks; canned goods; colander; cooky cutter; egg beater; funnel; kettle; measuring spoons; pail; pan; pie plate; pie server; spatula; tray; wire strainer; aluminum pressure cooker canner; aluminum cooking and baking utensils; cooky and pastry press for professionalizing homemade cookies; 10-piece set of cooky molds; aluminum beverage service; omelet pan; rainbow-lacquered bowl set.

ELEVENTH—*Steel.*—All-steel equipment for home, office, garden; bread box; cake cover and tray; canister set; carving set, with steel; filing cabinet; folding chairs; hand tools; household scale; kitchen shears; kitchen stool; cutlery; lawn mower; pocketknife; fine scissors in case; three-tier shoe rack; stainless steel cookware and tableware; all-steel typing table; wardrobe; pinking shears; medicine cabinet; manicure set; and for the gift of a lifetime for those who like to putter around the work bench, a steel chest of fine tools.

TWELFTH—*Linen, Silk, and Nylon.*—Irish linen damask for formal and informal occasions; buffet and bridge cloths in rich colors (monograms to order); linen bedspreads, with fine Madeira cutwork and embroidery; tea napkins, hand embroidered; Irish linen napkins, with hand-drawn hemstitching; Irish linen towelling, designed for doilies, napkins, curtains, aprons; and tea towels; linen china, glass, platter, tea and hand towels; linen handerchiefs; silk and nylon lingerie and stockings; curtains, gloves; set of silk-covered hangers; dresser drawer set; handkerchiefs; lamp and candle shades; silk negligee; paisley suit scarf; pajamas; shower coat; pillow; umbrella; silk comforter.

THIRTEENTH—*Lace.*—Antimacassar; blouse; bureau scarf; chair back and arm protectors; china dolls in lace ruffs; collar and cuff set in real Honiton lace; plate doilies, with lace edges; hat veiling; curtains; dress; evening shawl; gloves and mitts; real lace handkerchief; neckwear; runners and doilies for dressers, vanities, and night tables; insertion and lace edging by the yard; lace flouncing; tablecloth; heirloom lace bedspread.

FOURTEENTH—*Ivory.*—Any imported curio of carved ivory; tiny ivory elephants; ivory-handled fruit, paper, or pen knives; jewel cases with inlaid ivory lids; beads and bracelets of carved ivory.

FIFTEENTH—*Crystal.*—Antique candelabra or lamp; bouquet and bud vases; cut-glass cake dishes; small dishes for conserves, salted nuts, and mints; decanters; toiletry ensembles in cut-glass bottles; goldfish in glass bowl; ornamental glass flowers, figurines, and animals; monogrammed crystal stemware; crystal glass punch bowl, with twelve handled cups and glass ladle; salad set, with serving bowl, eight glasses and silverplated salad-servers; glass console set for floral and fruit arrangements; mirrors; magnifying, reading, and sun glasses; glass ovenware; glass tableware.

TWENTIETH—*China.*—Complete dinner, lunch, and tea sets in antique and modern chinaware; meat platter; china bowls; after-dinner coffee cups; teapots; porcelain china electric clock; Chinese rose quartz teapots; tidbit tray, made of three pottery plates on a brass handle; Wedgwood vases, urns, and decorative plates for hanging; pairs of Chinese men brilliantly glazed; Dresden china museum pieces; tiny china cats, dogs, horses, pitchers, shoes, cup-and-saucer sets in famous makes.

TWENTY-FIFTH—*Silver.*—Candelabra; candlesticks; cake basket; card case; charms; cigarette case; sterling silver dresser sets; dressing case, with silver-topped containers; entree dish; flatware; silver frame that folds and snaps shut, for traveling bag, handbag, desk or dressing table; fruit bowl; fruit knives; hand bell; for men, sterling silver identification bracelet, tie holder, bill clip, key chain, belt buckle; for women, cutout monogram pin, solid earrings, dangle bracelet; jewel case; silver-backed military brushes; pie knife with sterling handle; sandwich plate; set of sterling buttons; souvenir spoons; sugar tongs; trays; vases; silver tea or coffee service, with tray.

THIRTIETH—*Pearl.*—Any mother-of-pearl or oyster shell novelty; evening clutch bag, hand-embroidered with mock pearls; inlaid binoculars; dress combs; fruit knives; fountain pens; boxes with mother-of-pearl inlay; sunshades, umbrellas, canes with mother-of-pearl handles; pearl costume jewelry; string of genuine pearls.

THIRTY-FIFTH—*Coral.*—Coral novelties from marine displays in curio and souvenir shops; jewelry, especially necklaces, or real coral.

FORTIETH—*Ruby.*—Ruby-colored glass bowls, vases;

crystal beads in ruby color; set of fine costume jewelry in ruby-set gold.

FORTY-FIFTH—*Sapphire.*—Trays, souvenirs, and jewelry made of sapphire-colored flowers; vases and ornaments of sapphire-blue glass; strings of sapphire crystal beads; costume jewelry of mounted sapphires.

FIFTIETH—*Golden.*—New group picture of the great-grandchildren or of the newest baby in a solid gold frame; gold-mounted magnifying glass; bedside hand bell; gold-lidded glass container for sweets, cookies, etc.; "Golden Hour" mystery clock, with a face of solid brass in a circle of gold, and two slim golden hands seemingly floating in space; a gift of money in a gold embossed box.

FIFTY-FIFTH—*Emerald.*—Green plastic or glass trees, flowers, animals, figurines; lapel pin of jeweled shamrock; complete set of distinctive costume jewelry of imitation emeralds.

SEVENTY-FIFTH—*Diamond.*—Many of the gifts suggested for the crystal anniversary are suitable for the diamond; rhinestone jewelry; gifts with "diamond"-studded initials; genuine diamond earrings.

BEATRICE PLUMB

Traditions and Symbols

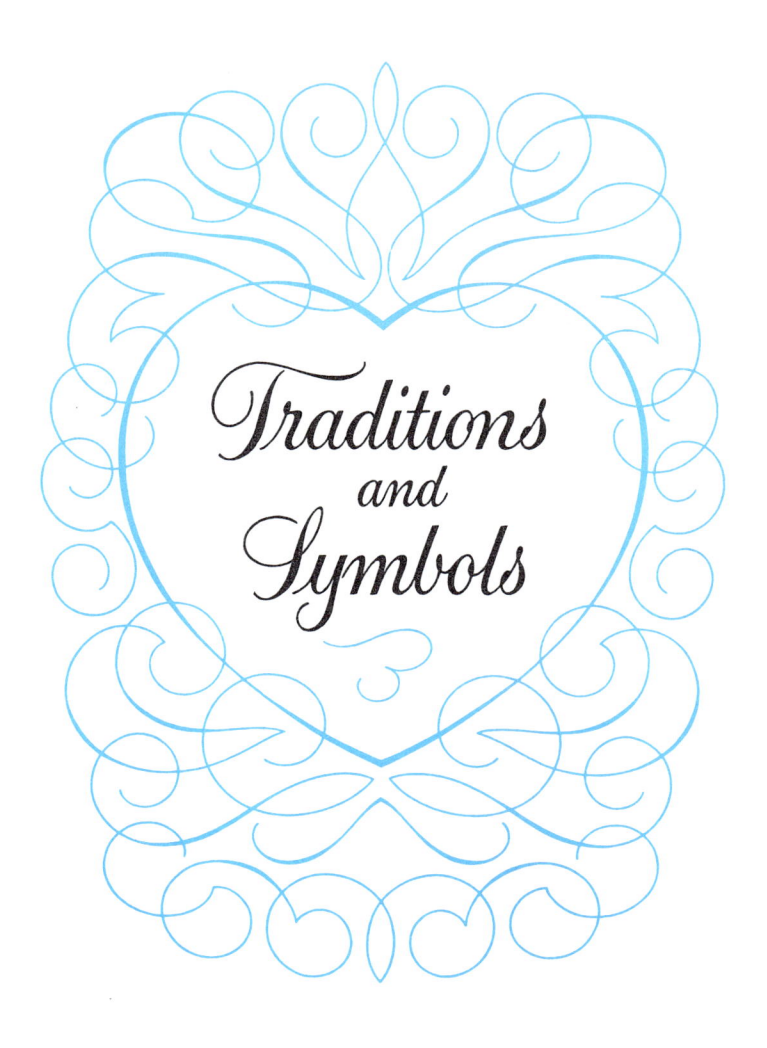

Marry Monday, marry for wealth;
Marry Tuesday, marry for health;
Marry Wednesday, the best day of all;
Marry Thursday, marry for crosses;
Marry Friday, marry for losses;
Marry Saturday, no luck at all.
OLD NURSERY RHYME

Marry in May, repent away.
Marry in Lent, live to repent.
ENGLISH PROVERBS

The diamond ENGAGEMENT RING first started in Italy during the Middle Ages. But giving a ring as a symbol of a pledge to wed probably goes back to the days of bride purchase. Pledge rings have been made of braided grass, the hair of the loved one woven into a lover's knot, leather and metal. Among the early Anglo-Saxons, a ring was placed on the woman's right hand, and shifted to the left at the marriage ceremony.

The wearing of the WEDDING RING on the left fourth finger is due to the ancient belief that the vein ran from that finger directly to the heart. But wedding rings were worn on the thumb among English women during Elizabethan times, and is worn on the right hand to this day in many foreign countries. Wedding rings go back to Egyptian times and their circular shape symbolizes unending love.

The BRIDAL VEIL is usually assumed to be a symbol of purity, hiding the face of the "blushing bride". Actually, it may have been a sign of submission. This symbolic meaning is still existant in some Church orders, where a woman "takes the veil" to suggest her obedience to the order's